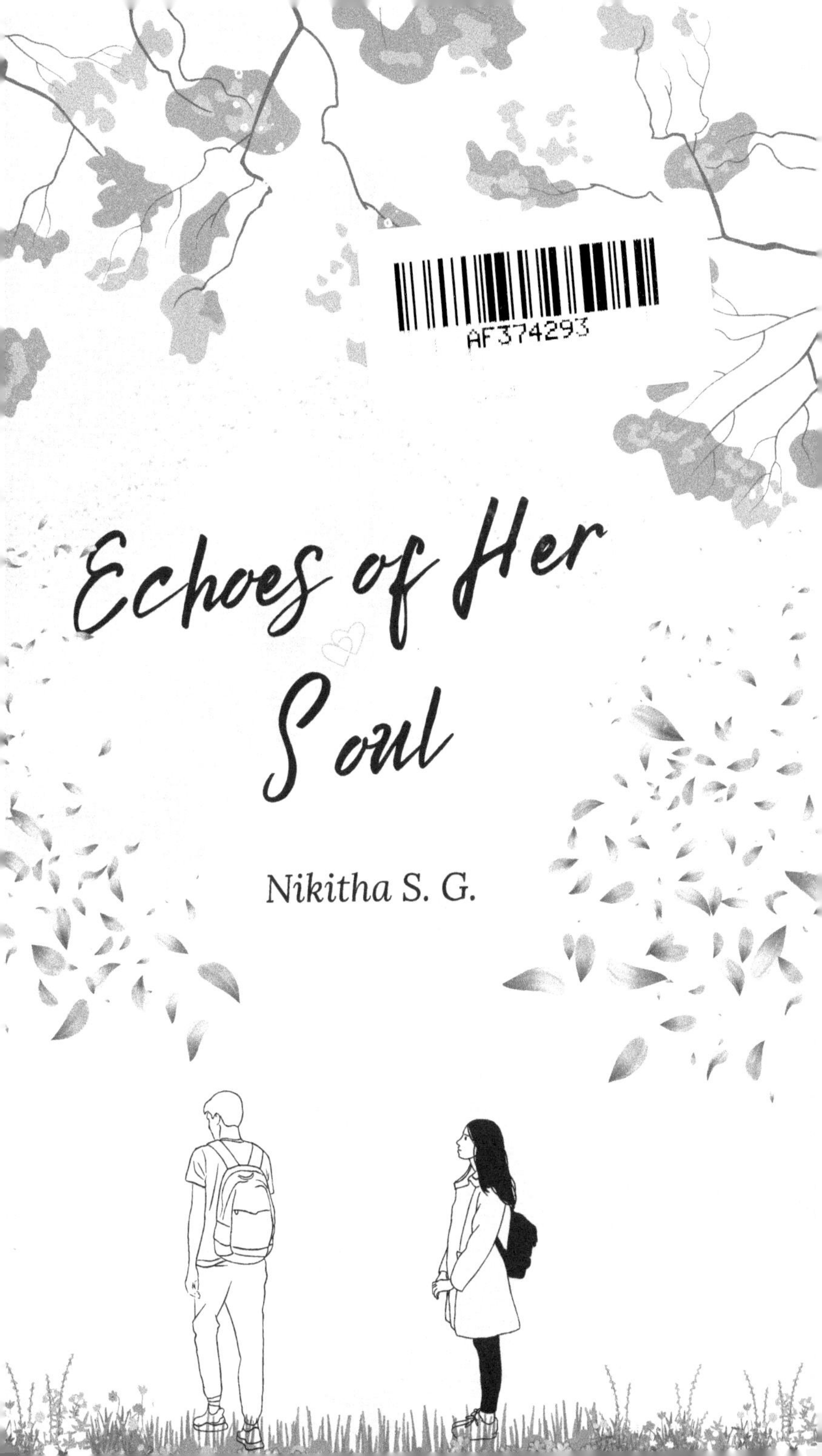

Echoes of Her Soul

Nikitha S. G.

Embracing the Unknown

She ventured forth beneath the foreign skies,

A pilgrim drawn to wisdom's distant flame.

With courage bright, reflected in her eyes,

She treaded paths unknown, devoid of name.

Within her stirred a storm of silent dreams,

Yet anchored by resolve, she moved ahead.

Each step dismantled doubt's entangled seams,

New truths replaced old fears that she had shed.

Her quest was more than learning's ample store,

She longed to breathe the air of liberty.

To cast away the chains she knew before,

And grow beneath a sky where she'd be free.

Thus, far from home, her heart began to bloom,

In lands anew, her spirit found its room.

Soul's Awakening

In dreams she reached, aspiring heights untold,

A heart aflame, compassion in her hold.

To serve the poor, uplift the ones who ache,

And heal the earth, her soul's own mandate.

For parents dear, she yearned a life serene,

A haven safe, where joy and love convene.

Selfless, she stood, her focus on their bliss,

A daughter's wish, their happiness the gist.

But lo, a man appeared within her days,

Who taught her how to love in myriad ways.

He showed the path to self-discovery,

Unveiling truths, love's profound alchemy.

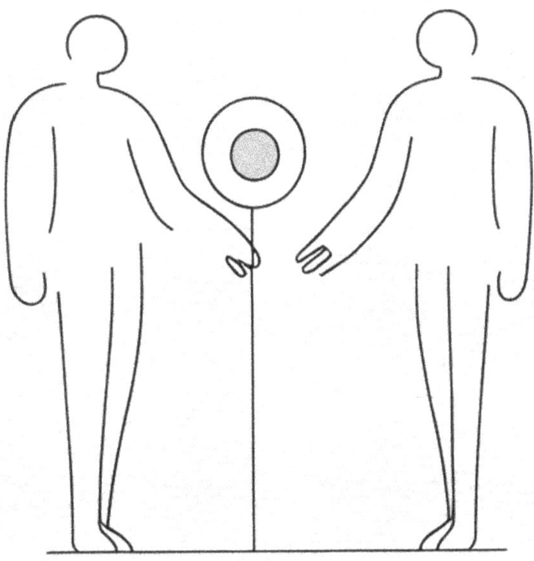

Through him, she learned the essence pure and true,

A love that binds, transforms her spirit, too.

Fated Sight

A chance encounter, destiny's decree,

In darkness met, yet hearts began to see.

Amidst the pool's allure, their voices wove,

A friendship born, uncharted depths to probe.

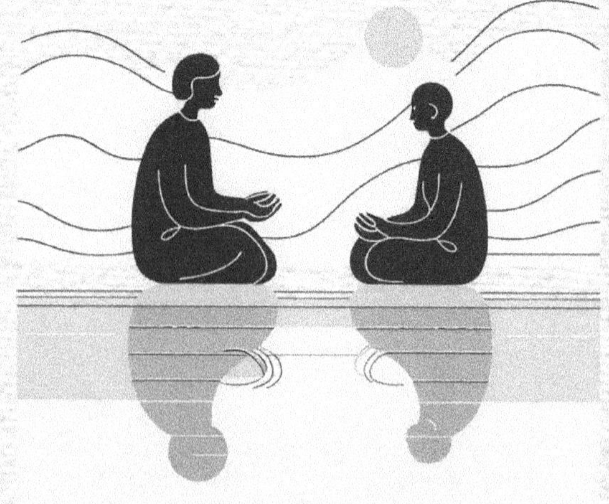

"Nice to meet you," she spoke with hopeful grace,

Though sightless, laughter danced within the space.

No spark ignited, or so it seemed that day,

Yet little did they know what fate would sway.

Just strangers met, a fleeting rendezvous,

A glimpse of what the future had in view.

No inkling of the love that lay in store,

A bond unspoken, waiting to explore.

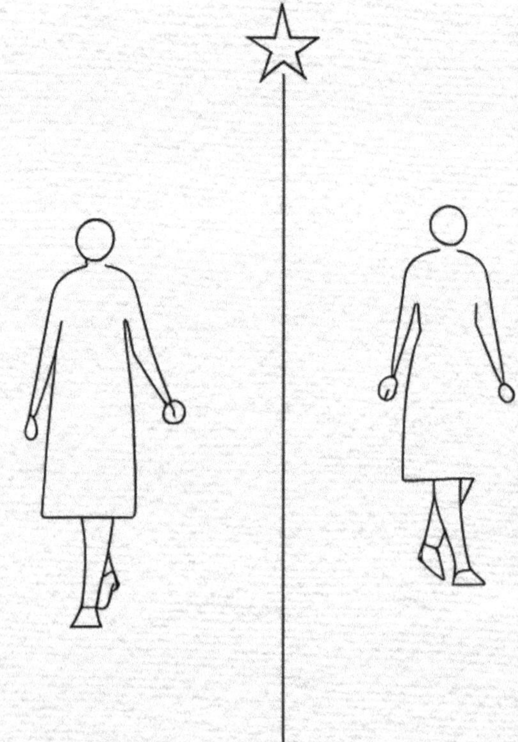

Oh, strange meeting, where sight was cast aside,

A tale of love that destiny did hide.

Whispered Affection

In friendships formed, a bond began to grow,

Through trips and laughter, spirits intertwined.

But subtle shifts arose, a gentle flow,

Thoughts of him lingered, whispered in her mind.

At first, she pushed away, denied the fire,

Love's spectre looming feared its sweet hold.

For she had never sought such strong desire,

Preferring solitude, her private space.

Yet, in the depths, affection gently bloomed,

Unbidden feelings, like a fragrant bloom.

She fought against the pull, with all her might,

To keep her heart unburdened, free from doom.

But love prevailed, relentless and sincere,

Her heart's resistance broken, love held dear.

Relentless Battle

In the depths of her soul, a turmoil brewed,

A battle fought, emotions unsubdued.

She scorned herself for thoughts she could not tame,

Love's tendrils, ever-growing, stoked the flame.

Her dreams and aspirations held no sway,

For in her heart, his presence held its stay.

She raged against the current, tried to flee,

Yet destiny's design had set her free.

Self-hatred gnawed upon her weary soul,

She sought to mask her feelings, take control.

Distractions sought, to quell love's potent call,

But fate, unyielding, laughed and watched her fall.

Defeated, she acknowledged her truth at last,

Love's sweet surrender, her heart held steadfast.

Heart's Crossroad

A heart divided, uncertain in its quest,

To follow love's path or heed caution's behest.

Encouragement and warning clash within,

Her mind entangled in a web of sin.

No prior love, no guideposts to avail,

She wanders lost, in confusion's dark veil.

Seeking the name for feelings yet unknown,

A love pure and selfless, to be shown.

She ponders, can she love without demands,

Bestow her all with no set expectations?

Or is it mere attraction's fleeting dance,

That fades with time, a shallow infatuation?

Within this turmoil, she seeks the truth,

The name for feelings, hidden in her youth.

Love's Quandary

In shadows cast by doubts, her heart entwined,

A best friend's guidance, a glimmer to find.

Take that first step, to destiny surrender,

Discover truths that fate has yet to render.

His care, his words, they resonate so deep,

But friendship's boundary makes her heart weep.

She yearns for more, a love beyond compare,

Yet fears the pain if he's not truly there.

She tells herself, his love is not required,

Her own devotion is all that's desired.

But why does jealousy claw within her chest,

When he draws close to others she knows best?

His presence, like a moonbeam's gentle glow,

Yet doubts and assumptions torment her so.

Defiant Symphony

In depths of doubt, her soul in sorrow drowns,

As questions haunt, her heart's desires bound.

For parents' ire, a hurdle to be faced,

To win their blessing, love's path must be traced.

If love it be, she yearns to make it known,

To hold him close, through life's journey alone.

Convincing them, a battle she'll engage,

Ready to face all struggles on love's stage.

For he, her soul's completion, perfect one,

Her cherished love, her moon, her shining sun.

His presence fills her life with pure delight,

With him, she feels her world set bright.

She'll fight for love, against the tides that roll,

In his soothing grasp, her heart has found its goal.

Fateful Proposal

With heart in hand, she braved the unknown tide,

To ask the question, her emotions wide.

No expectations held, she sought the truth,

To know his thoughts, the answers she pursued.

Assumptions lingered, casting doubt's dark spell,

Yet hope's small ember in her heart did dwell.

Proposing not for love, but for release,

A chance to move on, find her inner peace.

She approached, trembling, words at last unveiled,

Awaiting his response, love's truth unveiled.

Would he declare their bond, or just a friend?

Her heart prepared for a resounding end.

And as she asked, her voice a gentle plea,

His answer held the key, her destiny.

Heart's Turmoil

A quarter-hour, an eternity it seemed,

Anxious heart, a dream so long esteemed.

In warmth of shelter, they would finally meet,

For her to utter words, her soul's retreat.

Each passing second, like a decade worn,

Her heart in turmoil, trembling and forlorn.

Anticipation danced within her core,

As she prepared her soul for love's closed door.

And there, at last, the moment of their fate,

With quivering voice, her feelings she'd relate.

"I have feelings for you," her words did flow,

Bearing her heart's truth, her love to bestow.

In trembling hope, she sought his reply,

A truth unveiled, where love's fate would lie.

November's Limbo

November's embrace, three months have gone by,

Uncertainty lingers, questions in the sky.

He asks her choice, if yes or if it's no,

But he can't answer yet, his heart in tow.

Not ready for love, he pleads for some time,

To sort his thoughts, to find his heart's true rhyme.

No clear expression of what lies within,

Leaves her in limbo, hopes and doubts akin.

He offers friendship, a balm for her soul,

To move on, seek peace, and make her heart whole.

Yet, she ponders if this choice is right,

To keep him close, yet not hold love too tight.

In friendship's realm, they'll tread with no regret,

Unveiling love's truth, the path they've met.

Hope's Flickering

In awkward moments, she finds solace lost,

His presence lingers, at what cost?

He promised friendship, a familiar ground,

But doubts and questions still doth resound.

His reaction, analyzed by others' voice,

Just kindness shown, no room for love's choice.

But deep within her heart, a flicker stays,

Hope's gentle flame, refusing to displace.

Out of his league, she tells herself true,

No place for love, a fact she must construe.

Yet thoughts persist, he asked for time to find,

A future where their hearts might intertwine.

Awkwardness surrounds, her mind debates,

A sonnet of uncertainty, love awaits.

Heart's Memoir

She vowed to move on, her heart's desire waned,

Distraction sought, in art and work ingrained.

A rejection claimed, though not overtly shown,

Manipulating truth, a shield she's grown.

Creating memories, moments to treasure,

As friends, they'd share, their bond to measure.

Yet his distance lingers, a silent ache,

A yearning heart, for more connection's sake.

Mixed emotions swirl, a tumultuous sea,

Happy moments marred by melancholy.

His presence, a boon, completes her day,

While longing for more, her heart does sway.

In this delicate dance of hope and friend,

Their story unfolds, with no certain end.

Thanksgiving's Grace

Amidst the autumn's grace, they journeyed on,

Within Virginia's arms, where dreams are drawn.

Excitement filled the air, hearts all aligned,

Longest hours spent; memories enshrined.

Every action noted, imprinted deep,

Each word he utters, her heart does keep.

But friends, mischievous, their teasing reigns,

Awkwardness, she fears, in his soul it stains.

Her pleas in vain, their laughter still prevails,

Their knowing glances, like playful gales.

Yet he, composed, his thoughts steady and clear,

A friend he sees, with no shadows of fear.

Thanksgiving's grace, a trip to remember,

Their shared moments, love's embered ember.

Euphoric Waves

Beneath the morning sky, they walked the shore,

Unintentional encounter, fate's gentle chore.

A sunrise beckoned, painting colors bright,

In nature's arms, her soul took flight.

Unaware, he strolled with carefree delight,

While she, enraptured, bathed in love's pure light.

Waves whispered secrets, soothing hearts entwined,

A symphony of peace, in harmony aligned.

For him, another day, for her, much more,

Euphoria engulfed, an ocean's roar.

In footsteps shared, a precious memory,

A treasured moment, etched in reverie.

The sunrise witnessed love, unspoken, true,

A heart adrift, in a world born anew.

Love's Boundlessness

In the realm of seasons, Spring has arrived,

Yet whispers of uncertainty reside.

Five months remain, and time slips through her grasp,

Will she withstand the absence of his clasp?

A longing stir, her heart yearning to be near,

For without his presence, she feels unclear.

A week apart feels like an eternity,

The ache of longing, a constant plea.

But as a friend, she finds solace and bliss,

Love knows no bounds; in any form it exists.

To have his company, even from afar,

Brings warmth to her soul, like a guiding star.

Yet worries loom, of fading memories,

She prays their bond endures life's mysteries.

Tangled Longing

Upon her heart, the fear of him departing,

A haunting nightmare, relentless in its hold.

She hides her longing, her soul quietly smarting,

Avoiding him, emotions left untold.

Their paths may cross, but only by sheer chance,

He keeps his distance, never drawing near.

Their friendship dwells in an unyielding dance,

The growing void between them, crystal clear.

She ponders how she'll bear his absence keen,

For he won't call or send a message true.

Her heartache lingers, questioning unseen,

Why does she yearn for him, her heart askew?

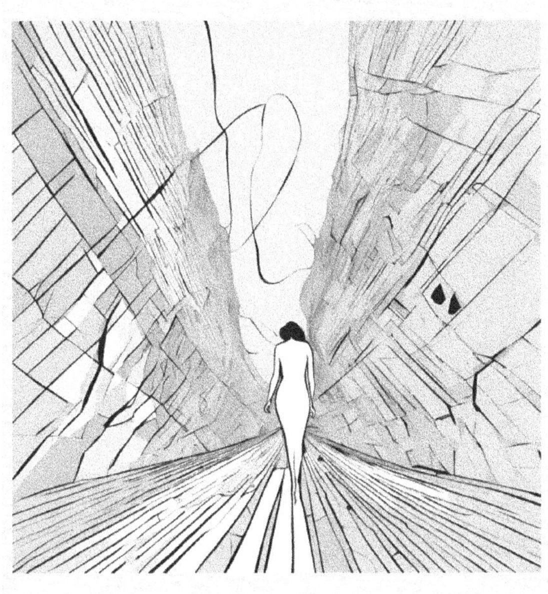

In confusion's grip, she wanders astray,

No sage advice to guide her on her way.

Navigating Love's Labyrinth

Lost in the maze of unrequited love,

She searches for a path, a guiding light.

The trap of youth, "situationships" thereof,

Leaves her and friends entangled in their plight.

As an adult, she longs for sage advice,

But finds her friends are tangled just the same.

Inexperienced, her heart pays the price,

Unsure if she should stay or break the chain.

She ponders if her yearning is misplaced,

A prisoner to emotions undefined.

Her heart, entwined, her thoughts interlaced,

She yearns for clarity she cannot find.

Alone she stands, with questions left to roam,

Seeking answers, in this emotional home.

Bittersweet Rain

Upon a day so dreary, clouds hung low,

Their tears did fall, the atmosphere turned gray.

A gift she sought to hide, a friend to show,

But little did she know what lay astray.

Within his house, where warmth and comfort dwell,

He kindly asks her in, a rare invite.

A fleeting moment, but she feels a swell,

Mixed joy and sorrow, emotions alight.

Why does his courtesy bring such delight?

And yet, the sadness whispers in her mind,

For soon he'll leave, their time too brief, too slight,

Their paths diverging, fate unkind, unkind.

A paradox, her happiness in woe,

The fleeting joy, the bittersweet tableau.

Elusive Escape

Lost in thoughts of him, she sought escape,

Through bustling days and endless, sleepless nights.

Her schedule full, a hectic, frantic tape,

To bury feelings deep, keep out of sight.

Part-time jobs and coursework filled her days,

A desperate bid to banish his embrace.

But futile efforts met her weary gaze,

His presence lingered, stubbornly in place.

She questioned sanity, her mind askew,

Had she turned into a haunting, creeping ghost?

Obsessed, consumed, her thoughts focused askew,

A lovesick heart, a soul in desperate throes.

Yet deep down, she knew, it wasn't wrong,

To long for love, to sing his name in song.

Panic's Blaze

In her bustling life, no end in sight,

She missed the chance to glimpse his gentle face,

For the first time, his presence took her flight,

As if he were invisible in that space.

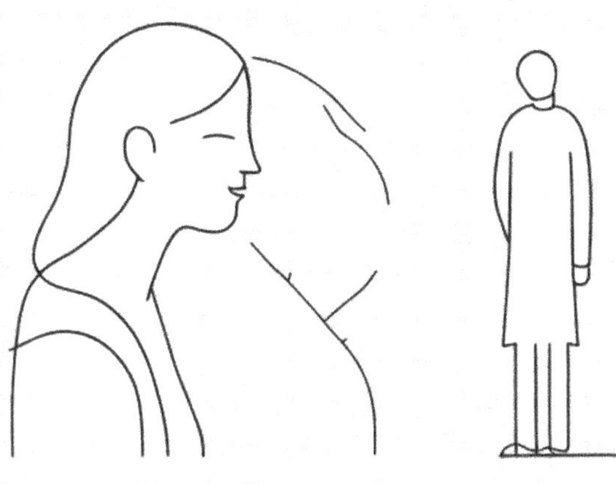

Her cold dismissal caused her heart to ache,

While she struggled on, just trying to survive,

Then he appeared, a common friend, a break,

But emotions raged, impossible to hide.

Her longing grew to be close, to draw near,

Yet in her efforts, she sought to retreat,

In vain she fought, her attempts did not clear,

His arrival stirred a tempest, bittersweet.

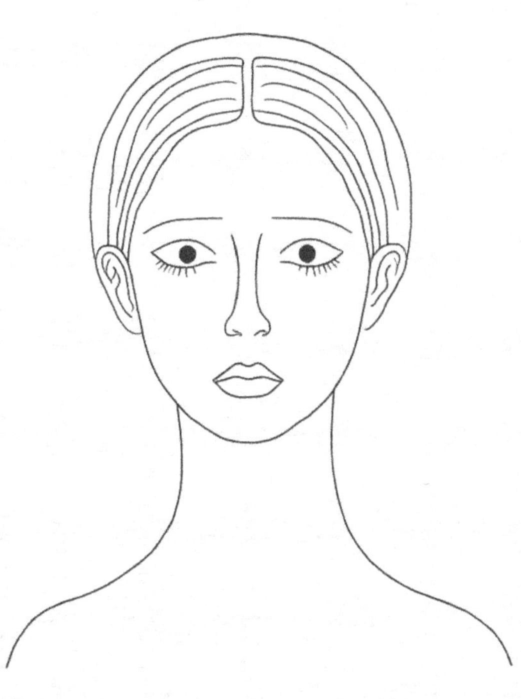

She couldn't bear to meet his piercing gaze,

Unknown emotions sparked her panic's blaze.

Farewell's Embrace

The day arrives, his leave draws near, we part,

Her heart's not ready, loath to see him go,

A couple of weeks, he'll soothe her woe,

Yet soon again, he'll bid goodbye, depart.

She knows it's final, ne'er to meet again,

No calls, no visits, lost in time's cruel swell,

Thoughts of their parting, hell's own tale they tell,

To be away, her soul can't bear the pain.

She hides in libraries, seeks solace there,

Refusing meetings, emotions running wild,

Overwhelmed, she fears her tears revealed,

But later, reason whispers in her ear.

Regret would haunt her if she did not try,

To say farewell, her heart she can't deny.

The Parting Moment

Her steps, though heavy, move towards his face,

The last goodbye, she dare not let unfold,

Her heart, a tempest, she cannot withhold,

But must control herself in this grim space.

She runs to seek her room's serene retreat,

To calm her soul before him she'll be seen,

To bid adieu and face the in-between,

Entering now this dark and sorrowed sheet.

With heavy heart, she stands before him now,

She's steeled her nerves, prepared to say farewell,

But seeing him, her resolution breaks,

Her tears flow free, her pain upon her brow.

Despite the hurt, she bids him her goodbye,

In agony, she parts with one last sigh.

Unrequited Connection

He knows her suffering, been through the same,

A text he sends after their parting's blow,

"How are you?" asked with care, yet she lies low,

Silence and ignorance her answer's claim.

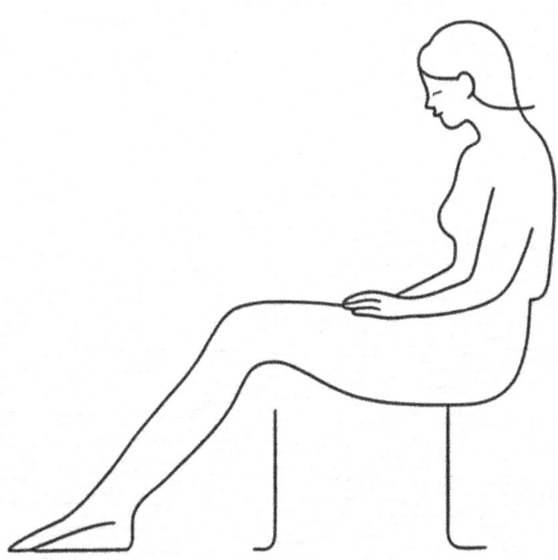

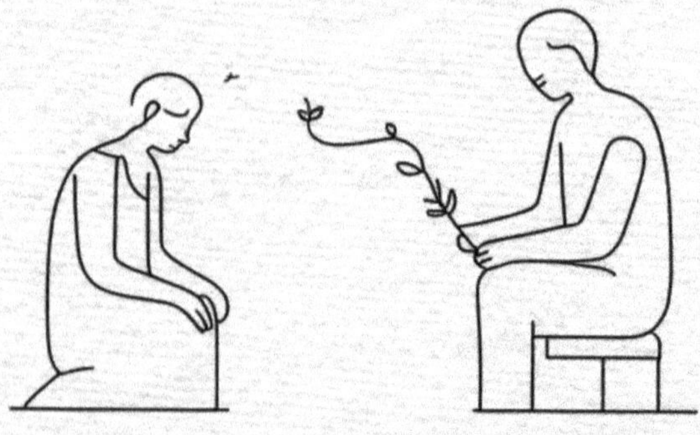

Not wanting falsehood, nor emotions shown,

She bears the weight of her feelings inside,

Though he perceives the pain she can't abide,

He talks to soothe, her soul to mend, to own.

His kindness all she seeks, nothing beyond,

No lifelong love, nor his time to hold,

Just simple touch, his words, a story told,

A friend departed, through messages fond.

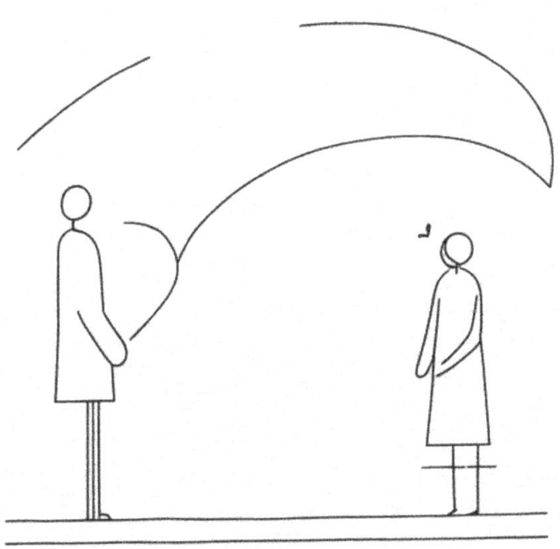

Expectations bruise her heart, she contends,

Yet love without them, she seeks, transcends.

Love Unconditionally

In touch they keep, but fleeting are those ties,

His texts, mere moments of compassion's art,

A day or two, they speak, then drift apart,

Her hopes restrained, though love within her lies.

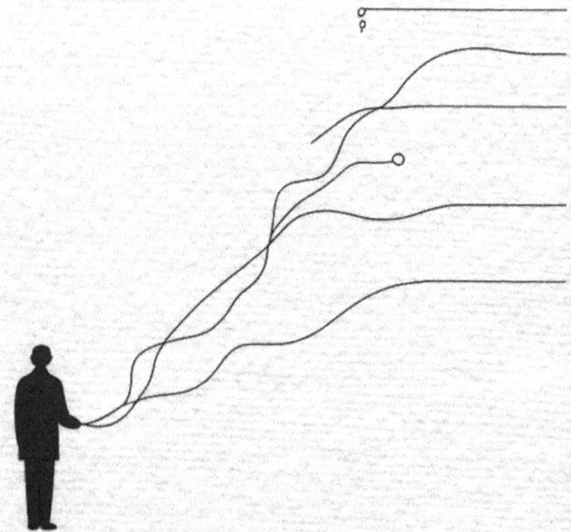

Unconditional love, her heart's true plea,

Where pain finds not a home, only delight,

In selfless grace, love's pure and joy takes flight,

But human nature struggles to be free.

She shan't give up, for possibilities,

Though far and wide, love's journey may extend,

Her love without expectations won't bend.

A quest for love that blossoms, boundless, free,

Through trials and tears, till the end she'll find,

In love's embrace, true solace for her mind.

Fleeting Memories

He's back, but only for a day to stay,

Far away he'll go, leaving her behind,

A day of memories that millions find,

Etched in her heart, for life, they'll hold their sway.

An evening spent with friends, he came along,

They asked for answers he failed to give,

To clear confusion, doubts that made her grieve,

In midnight's hour, truth would right the wrong.

Their talk began, with normal words exchanged,

But soon he asked about her heart's decree,

Her answer clear, she hasn't moved on, see,

He explained why his soul still lay estranged.

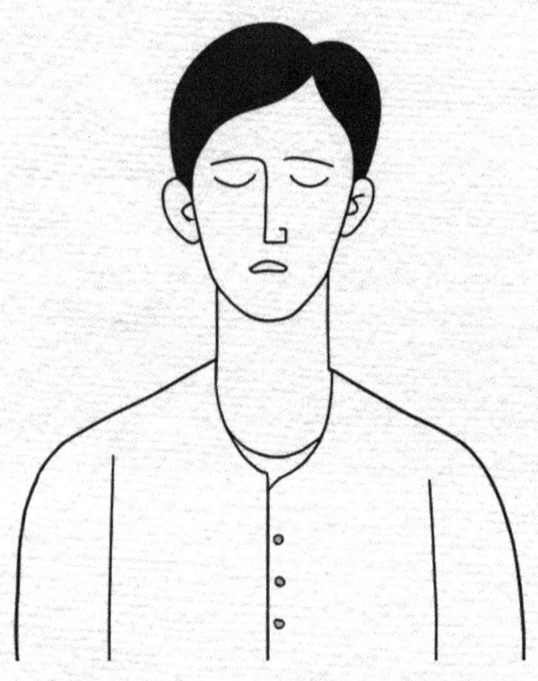

Not yet emerged from loss, his heart's confined,

He fears commitment, love yet undefined.

Depths of Uncertainty

He's not disliking her, he softly said,

But fear of love's commitment holds him tight,

In grief, his heart remains, a starless night,

Uncertain, tangled thoughts inside his head.

He feels unworthy, wasting her life's breath,

Yet she insists, she'll wait forevermore,

Her heart devoted, patient to the core,

Her love, a solace for his soul in death.

He's not prepared to lead her heart astray,

Until he finds the closure he must seek,

And so, he leaves her heart feeling meek,

Uncertainty remains the price to pay.

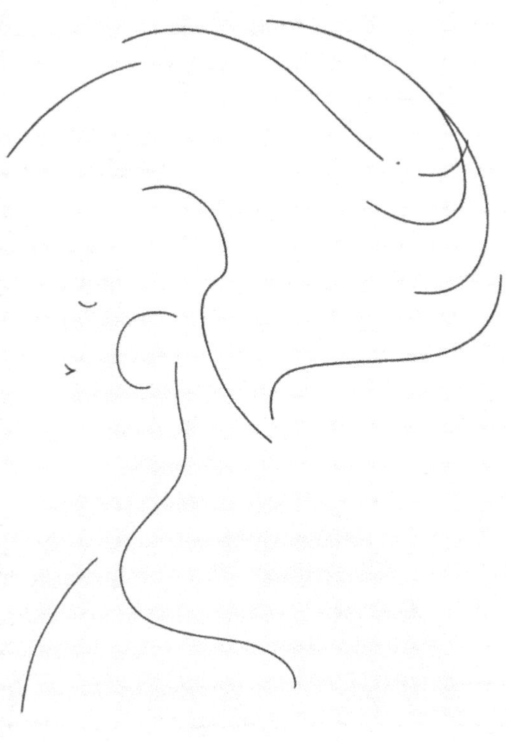

Amidst the doubts, she glimpses truth's faint glow,

A chance remains when he's prepared to show.

Hug of Comfort

The meet concludes, uncertain still the way,

Assumptions shattered, clarity revealed,

His words were honest, though her heart once reeled,

He cares, she knows, that message will not sway.

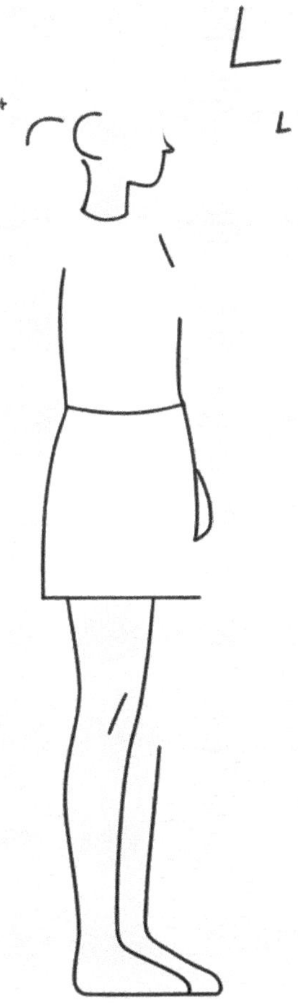

A hug they share, the one she longed to feel,

Embrace of home and heaven intertwined,

In that moment, hearts and souls aligned,

A tender touch that made her wounds to heal.

Their paths may part, but hope sustains her heart,

She'll cherish memories they hold so dear,

And if fate wills, they'll meet without a fear,

For love's uncertain, yet it's still an art.

With poised heart, she seeks "yes" or "no" aligned,

When free from past's binds, his certainty will find.

Emotions' Flight

With days aglow, a reason yet unclear,

Does he now care, at least as a dear friend?

Her happiness, a joy she can't transcend,

A high of emotions, bright and sincere.

Since they first met, such bliss she's never known,

Like dreams fulfilled, a heart on cloud nine soars,

Daily he talks, her soul's delight restores,

More than she asked, his care like seeds well sown.

But doubts intrude, she fears this joy won't stay,

For life's a mix of joy and sorrow's shade,

Yet in this moment, happiness displayed,

She'll cherish now, come what may on the way.

With hope in heart and dreams in skies unfurled,

In joy, she finds a glimpse of a new world.

Yearn and Seek

As fleeting as it came, his presence waned,

His texts diminished, leaving her forlorn,

She calls, he answers, still, a friendship's born,

Yet deep inside, her soul's yearning remained.

Missed his voice, appearance, all he shared,

Her heart desired his presence to hold near,

Not just a friend, she saw, much more, it's clear,

Emotion stirred, a truth she now declared.

She asked for friendship, sought him to be near,

But seeing the gap between her hope's embrace,

Her heart sought solace, longing for his face,

To move on's path, the only way is clear.

With love intact, she'll let him go, she'll find,

A love that endures, though hope's left behind.

Road to Letting Go

He tried to distance, she sought to be close,

In friendship's guise, she yearned for something more.

Expecting more than friendship could restore,

Her heart confused, the truth it must expose.

Between the lines, his feelings hard to trace,

A clear-cut "no" she wished for, to move on,

Her hope afloat, his silence lingers on,

His unclear answer, keeping love's chase.

To let him go, she'll brave a hopeful heart,

Not stop loving, yet release her hold tight,

She longs for closure, truth to bring to light,

A love that lingers, waiting for a start.

In loving him, she'll find her strength to cope,

A journey to let go, embracing hope.

Heart's Plea

In words of force, she sought his clear reply,

To say "no," the only path she'd pursue,

Peace in her heart, free from hope's strong ado,

With no expectations, her soul could fly.

She asked him, earnest, "Reject me," she pled,

An unprecedented plea to make,

For closure's sake, her heart's own truth to take,

No crosswords, just a simple "no" she said.

But why he never said those two small letters?

"No" seemed so elusive, hard to embrace,

His feelings veiled, love's presence to erase,

Her heart longed for it, seeking peace unfetters.

She takes his lack of words as her release,

Yet truth obscured, her heart seeks clarity's peace.

Unexpected Reality

Reality or manipulation's art,

She sought the rejection she longed to find,

Yet different from what dwelled in her mind,

Lost forever, his memory tears apart.

As if her loss was death, forever gone,

In struggles and sadness, she'll not be there,

Tears flowing, mind void, life feels unfair,

Emptiness grips her heart from dusk to dawn.

Uncontrollable tears down her cheeks stream,

Thoughts void, emptiness consumes her soul,

He gave her firsts, love's ebb and flow took toll,

Dull and gloomy, life becomes a dream.

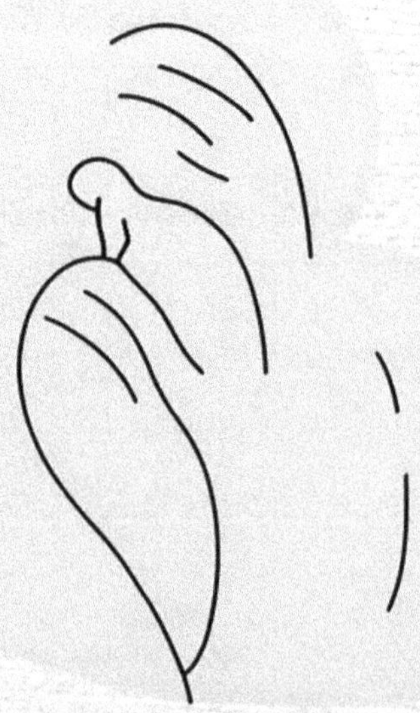

In the entrance of hell, nights take a toll,

Yet morning brings strength, her heart to console.

Surviving the Night

Few days, alcohol eased her heavy heart,

But strength she finds to face each passing night,

Dying, reborn with morning's dawning light,

A mantra whispered, "This too shall depart."

Letting go, she finds, can bring release,

His first love, forever in her heart,

No regrets, good memories' precious art,

Life's sad events, her strength they increase.

With new people and deeds, she seeks to mend,

Creating memories to fill the void,

Surviving, hoping for love's sweet reward,

Euphoria's touch, once more, her heart to send.

Becoming stronger, independent, she strides,

Yet that unknown feeling, her mind abides.

Unfolding Hopes

A month has passed, his ghost still lingers near,

New encounters, new paths she now explores,

Replacing memories, old wounds she shores,

A better self, each day, she strives to steer.

Seeking euphoria, in days ahead,

Unknown feeling remains a mystery,

She hopes, one day, it will no longer be,

Understanding, with time's wisdom fed.

Her love, a blessing, in his life, she dreams,

A wish for happiness, forever strong,

His memory's shadow, though it may long,

The future beckons, brighter than it seems.

For the one she awaits, strong, independent,

Love's journey onward, life transcendent.